Arduino

The ultimate guide to Arduino, including projects, programming tips & tricks, and much more!

Table of Contents

Introduction 1

Chapter 1: What Is Arduino 2

Chapter 2: The Different Arduino Models 10

Chapter 3: Getting Started With Arduino 19

Chapter 4: How To Code For Arduino 27

Chapter 5: Simple Arduino Projects You Can Try Out 34

Conclusion 43

Introduction

Thank you for choosing this book.

If you are interested in getting hands-on knowledge that will allow you to build your own Arduino projects, but you do not know where to start, this book is for you!

There is a common myth that building exciting projects with Arduino is a complicated affair, especially if you do not have any prior experience with electronics and programming. This books debunks that myth by guiding you through everything you need to know in order for you to start creating with Arduino.

In this book, you will learn quite a lot, including what Arduino is, why Arduino is the go-to platform for building electronics projects, the components of your Arduino, what you can use your Arduino for, the differences between various models of Arduino, and how to setup the Arduino programming environment and install drivers. This book will also show you how to create your first Arduino sketch, as well as some simple but interesting projects you can build using your Arduino, even if you have never written a single line of code before. The best part is that instead of using complex jargon, this book describes everything in simple and clear language that is perfect for absolute beginners!

Let's get started…

Chapter 1: What Is Arduino

In this chapter, you are going to learn about Arduino, what it is, what it does, what you get on the board and some of the advantages of using Arduino.

If computing and tech are among your interests, then you will definitely have heard about Arduino, a DIY platform that has become hugely popular among computing and electronics enthusiasts and hobbyists. Even if you are not much of a computing enthusiast, you might have come across the term Arduino in your online travels. So, what is the Arduino?

Arduino is basically an open source platform that can be used as the basis for all kinds of electronics projects. Arduino is made up of two major elements. The first element is a programmable physical circuit board, which is also known as a microcontroller. The second element is the Integrated Development Environment (IDE), which is software that you install on your computer. The IDE allows you to write and upload program code to the microcontroller. I mentioned that the Arduino board is programmable. This means that you can write computer programs that instruct the board on what to do. So, with the right set of instructions, you can program the Arduino to control any kind of hardware project. The Arduino board has the capability to read inputs – the press of a button, data from sensors, etc. – and generate an output – posting something online, switching on a LED light, activating a motor, etc. – based on the input.

The Arduino is the brain child of the Irvea Interaction Design Institute. It was conceptualized as a tool that would allow students with no prior background in programming and electronics to quickly prototype their projects. After its production, the wider community realized that Arduino was more adaptable to constantly changing needs and challenges in the field of electronics. The key behind its mass adoption was its versatility, since it can be used in all kinds of applications, from simple 8-bit boards to embedded environments, 3D printing, wearable electronic projects, and IoT projects. There's no limit to the kinds of projects you can build with Arduino.

Another reason behind Arduino's growth in popularity is that it set itself apart from the other programmable circuit boards that were in existence before its launch. With most other programmable circuit boards, you cannot load code to them without using special pieces of hardware known as programmers. However, Arduino does not require a programmer. You can simply load the code using an ordinary USB cable. Learning to use and program on Arduino is also quite easy. This is because Arduino uses an easy programming language that is derived from C++, one of the most popular programming languages.

Since its launch, Arduino has been used as the basis for numerous projects, from creating simple electronics, to complex scientific devices. It has also spawned a worldwide community of professionals, students, programmers, artists, and hobbyists around it. This community has generated tons of accessible information around the Arduino, making it a lot easier for beginner and experts alike to get the most out of their Arduino.

Arduino is an open source platform, which means that it is distributed under a CC-SA (Creative Commons Share-Alike) license. This means that anyone can modify the design and programming of the original Arduino board and distribute their new version to the public, provided they do it under the same CS-SA license. This provision has led to the creation of many different types of the Arduino board.

What Does The Arduino Do?

Arduino has many diverse applications. The platform was designed as an easy tool to help hackers, enthusiasts, hobbyists, designers, artists and newbies build interactive environments and devices. Arduino can interact with just about anything – the internet, LED's, cameras, TV's, physical buttons, smart phones and tablets, GPS devices, speakers, motors and much more. With this kind of flexibility, Arduino can be used as the brains behind all kinds of electronics projects, from building robots and smart locks to twitter enabled coffee makers and self-warming blankets.

Why Arduino?

There are several reasons as to why Arduino has found its way to thousands of projects around the world. The Arduino IDE is compatible with all common operating systems, including Windows, Mac, and Linux. The software is simple enough for learners, but flexible enough for more advanced users. Arduino has been used by teachers and students to get started with robotics and programming, to test physics and chemistry concepts, and to build low cost scientific instruments. Designers have used the device to come up with interactive prototypes, and musicians have used it to experiment with new instruments. Arduino has become an important platform through which people learn new things.

While there are several other microcontrollers available in the market, the benefits provided by Arduino have made it the most popular microcontroller platform. Some of the advantages of Arduino include:

- Inexpensive: One of the greatest advantage of Arduino boards is that they are very cheap. Whereas some microcontrollers will set you back a couple hundred dollars, you can pick up an Arduino board for about $15. Even if you go for a pre-assembled board, it is unlikely to cost you over $50. The low prices place the Arduino platform within reach of most people. It also makes it a lot easier to get another board and push on with your project in case you mess up and fry your board. It is not uncommon to make wrong wiring connections and fry your board, especially when you are just starting out.

- Cross-platform compatibility: The Arduino software will run perfectly on most common operating systems, unlike most other microcontroller systems which are only compatible with Windows.

- Easy to use: The Arduino Integrated Development Environment is very simple and clear. This means that even beginners who have had no prior experience with programming will have an easy time learning to program the Arduino board. At the same time, it is flexible enough to allow advanced users to build complex projects.

There's also a lot of Arduino tools and resources available, which makes it a lot easier and faster for beginners to start creating meaningful projects.

- Open source and extensible software: Since the Arduino platform is distributed under an open source license, it allows different people to create their own versions of the Arduino board, and to create and share their own projects. This helps expand the versatility of the Arduino even further.

What Is Included On The Board?

There are many different types of Arduino boards, all with different features and suited for different kinds of projects (this will be discussed more extensively in the next chapter). However, there are some components that are common among most types of Arduino boards. These include:

Power (USB/Barrel Jack)

For your Arduino board to work, it needs a source of power. Most Arduino boards can be powered either through the USB port or through the barrel jack. When using the USB port, the board will work well whether connected to a wall power socket or to a USB port on a computer. The USB port also allows you to load code onto your board. It's important to keep in mind that most Arduino boards have a recommended voltage of about 6 to 12 Volts. Do not connect your Arduino board to a power source that exceeds 20 Volts. This will overpower and fry your board.

Pins (5V, 3.3V, Digital, Analog, GND, AREF, PWM)

The Arduino board comes with pins that allow you to connect wires. This is essential since many projects will require you to create a circuit (you can easily do this using some wire and a breadboard). The pins usually have plastic headers, allowing you to simply plug the wire into the board. Different pins have different functions. Some of the most common pins include:

- 5V and 3.3V: These pins supply power to components connected to the Arduino board. As implied by the names, the 5V and 3.3V pins supply 5 and 3.3 volts of power respectively. This is the amount of power required by most of the simple components that you might need to connect to your board.

- Digital: These are a series of pins that are used for digital inputs and outputs. An example of a digital input is a physical push button. An example of a digital output is turning on a light bulb.

- Analog: These are a series of pins that you will find next to the 'Analog In' label. These pins are used for analog inputs. An example of an analog input is a pressure sensor. The analog pins read and convert input from analog devices into digital values.

- GND: These are a series of pins that you can use to ground your circuit.

- AREF: This is usually one pin known as the Analog Reference pin. In most cases, you might not need to use this pin. However, sometimes you can use it to set the upper limit for the analog input pins by connecting it to an external reference voltage.

- PWM: These series of pins are similar to the digital pins, though they are capable of something known as Pulse-Width Modulation (PWM). This means that they can be used to simulate analog outputs.

Reset Button

Most Arduino boards also come with a reset button. When you push the reset button, the reset pin gets temporarily connected to the ground. This restarts whatever code is loaded on your board. The reset button comes in handy when you want to test your code multiple times yet the code does not repeat.

LED Indicator

All Arduino boards come with a tiny but powerful LED light. You will find the word 'ON' written right next to the LED light. This LED light indicates the status of your Arduino board. Whenever you connect your board to a power source, the LED indicator should light up immediately. If you find that the LED indicator does not turn on after plugging in your board to a power source, this is an indication that something is wrong. You will need to re-check your circuit before proceeding.

TX RX LED's

TX is used to represent transmit, while RX represents receive. Most electronics will have the TX RX markings to show the pins that are involved in serial communication. On the Arduino board, these markings appear twice. You will find them next to the digital pins as well as next to two LED's. These are the TX RX LED's. The function of these LED's is to provide you with visual feedback whenever your board is transmitting or receiving data. For instance, the LED's will light up as you load new code onto your board.

Main IC

On all Arduino boards, you will find a large black component with several metal legs. This is known as the main IC, or main Integrated Circuit. While each Arduino board has a main IC, they do not all use the same main IC. Each board type uses a slightly different main IC. However, the main ICs on most Arduino boards are from ATMEL's ATmega line. It's important to know the type of IC on your board (as well as your board type), since the IDE might require you to choose your board and IC type before loading up a new program on the board. You can find this information by checking the top side of the IC.

Voltage Regulator

Arduino boards also include a voltage regulator, though this is not something that you are actually going to interact with. However, it's always good to know that it is there and what its function is. Like the name suggests, the voltage regulator regulates the amount of voltage getting into your board. It acts as a gatekeeper, letting through only enough voltage to keep the board running properly and preventing excess voltage that might fry your board. However, the voltage regulator has its limits. If you connect your board to a power source exceeding 20 volts, the voltage regulator won't be able to save your board.

Chapter Summary

In this chapter, you learned:

• Arduino is basically an open source platform that can be used as the basis for all kinds of electronics projects.

• Arduino is made up of two major elements, a programmable physical circuit board and the Integrated Development Environment (IDE).

• Arduino was conceptualized as a tool that would allow students with no prior background in programming and electronics to quickly prototype their projects.

• Arduino is an open source platform, which means that anyone can modify the design and programming of the original Arduino board and distribute their new version to the public.

• Arduino is very flexible, and is capable of interacting with just about anything.

• Arduino has been used on thousands of projects owing to its low cost, cross-platform compatibility, ease-of-use and its open source and extensible software.

• Some of the main components of an Arduino board include the power jack, pins, reset button, a LED indicator, TX RX LEDs, a main IC and a voltage regulator.

In the next chapter you will learn the differences between Arduino models.

Chapter 2: The Different Arduino Models

In this chapter, you are going to learn about the different models of the Arduino board and the differences between them.

Ever since the invention of Arduino in 2004, many versions of the board have been produced and sold. In addition, many other versions of the Arduino board have been developed by people outside the Arduino team. With all this, choosing the right Arduino board for your project can be a challenge. I am going to look at the features and designs of some common Arduino models to help you make a more informed decision on the best Arduino board for your needs.

It is good to note that despite all the different types of Arduino boards, some features and specifications are common to almost all models. Apart from the common features discussed in the previous chapter, most Arduino models use ATMEL's ATMEGA AVR series of microcontrollers.

It's also good to keep in mind that because there are several models of the Arduino board on the market, there are some classifications that are used to group together similar models. These classifications are based on factors like:

- Processing capabilities: One way of telling apart different kinds of Arduino boards is to look at their processing capabilities. These include things like the bandwidth, the clock-speed and the amount of memory on the board. The processing capabilities are determined by the type of microcontroller chip used on the board. The microcontroller chip also determines the kind of software that can run on the board.

- Feature set: The second method of distinguishing between different kinds of Arduino boards is to look at their feature set. These are the elements that come with the board (apart from the microcontroller), including things such as LED lights, buttons, input and output pins, as well as the connectivity options available on the board (Ethernet, USB, and so on).

- Form factor: Finally, you can distinguish between different models of the Arduino by looking at their form factor. Since Arduino boards are used as a basis for building all kinds of projects, they come in several sizes and shapes.

With that out of the way, we can now take a look at some of the most common boards, their feature sets and their distinguishing characteristics.

Arduino Uno (R3)

This is one of the most popular versions of the Arduino. It is also a good option if you are just starting to experiment with Arduino boards. There are various versions of the Arduino Uno, with the R3 being the most recent version. The Arduino Uno uses the ATMEGA328 MCU microcontroller chip. This board comes with 14 digital I/O pins. Of these, 6 have pulse width modulation capabilities. It also comes with 6 analog input pins, a power jack, a USB port, a reset button, an ICSP header and a 16 MHz ceramic oscillator. Instead of the FTDI USB-to-serial driver chip, the Arduino Uno uses a programmed ATmega 16U2 chip to act as a USB-to-serial converter. In addition, the R3 comes with added SCL and SDA pins, an IOREF pin and another extra unconnected pin.

Arduino Due

The Arduino Due was the first Arduino board to use a 32-bit ARM core microcontroller chip. It uses the SMART SM3X8E ARM Cortex M3 controller made by Atmel. The Due comes with 54 digital input/output pins. Of these, 12 have pulse width modulation capabilities. It also comes with 12 analog inputs, 2 Digital to Analog Converters, an 84 MHz oscillator, 4 hardware serial ports, 2 TWI, a USB OTG port, an SPI header, a power jack, an erase button, a reset button and a JTAG header. One thing you should keep in mind when using the Arduino Due is that it uses 3.3V. If you provide power exceeding the 3.3V to the I/O pins, you might end up damaging your board.

Arduino Yun

This board uses the ATMEGA32U4 processor. The Arduino Yun supports a Linux distribution known as Linino, owing to the Atheros AR9331 chip that comes along the ATMEGA32U4. This Arduino model is quite advanced, with an Ethernet port and an in-built Wi-Fi adapter. It also comes with a micro SD card slot and USB-A port. This board has 12 analog input pins and 20 digital I/O pins. Of these, 7 have pulse width modulation capabilities. The Yun also comes with 3 reset buttons, an ICSP header, a micro USB port and a 16 MHZ crystal oscillator. Since the Yun comes with an onboard Linux distribution, it combines the ease of Arduino with a powerful networked computer.

Apart from using Linux commands on the Arduino Yun, it also allows you to write your own Python scripts and shell for more functional interactions. The ATMEGA32U4 processor on the Yun also provides USB communication, therefore this board does not require a secondary processor to handle USB communications. When you connect the Arduino Yun on your computer, it appears as both a keyboard and a mouse, as well as a virtual (CDC) serial port.

Arduino Micro

The ATMEGA32U4 powered Arduino Micro was built in collaboration with Adafruit. The Micro comes with 12 analog input pins and 20 digital I/O pins. Out of the 20, 7 have pulse width modulation capabilities. The Micro also comes with an ICSP header, a micro USB port, a 16 MHz crystal resonator, and a reset button. This board comes with everything required to support the microcontroller, therefore all you need to do is simply use the micro USB cable to your PC and you are good to go. In addition, its form factor is well suited for placement on a breadboard.

Arduino Robot

This model is quite interesting, especially when you consider that it is essentially an Arduino on wheels. The Arduino robot comes with two boards – a motor board and a control board – and a processor for each board. The motor board naturally controls the motors. The control board, on the other hand, reads data from the sensors and determines what should be done. The two boards use the ATMEGA32U4 processors and are both fully programmable. Just like the Arduino Yun, the Arduino Robot comes with in-built USB communication, making the configuration process quite easy. This also means that a secondary processor is not required.

Arduino Esplora

This board was derived from another Arduino board known as the Leonardo. The Arduino Esplora's microcontroller is powered by an ATMEGA32U4 processor. The Esplora was made for people who want to get started with Arduino without any prior knowledge of electronics.

The Esplora comes with several input sensors, including a light sensor, a microphone, a slider, an accelerometer, a temperature sensor and a joystick. It also comes with onboard light and sound outputs. You can expand the capabilities of the Arduino Esplora through the provided TFT LCD screen socket or through the two Tinkerkit I/O connectors.

Arduino Mega (2560)

This board is powered by the ATMEGA2560 CPU. It comes with 54 digital I/O pins and 16 analog input pins. 15 of the digital I/O pins have pulse width modulation capabilities. The Mega (2560) also comes with a USB port, 4 hardware serial ports, an ICSP header, a 16 MHz crystal resonator, a reset button and a power jack. This board is compatible with a wide variety of shields. To get started with the Arduino Mega, simply connect it to your PC via USB and you are good to go.

Arduino Mini

The Arduino Mini was initially designed to use the ATMEGA168 processor. However, it was later upgraded to use the ATMEGA328. The Mini is designed for use on breadboards as well as on projects with space limitations.

The Arduino Mini comes with 8 analog inputs and 14 digital I/O pins, with 6 being capable of pulse width modulation. It is also equipped with a 16 MHz crystal oscillator. To program the Arduino Mini, you can use the Rs232 to TTL serial adapter, the Serial USB adapter or the other USB.

LilyPad Arduino Board

This is an Arduino board that is designed for use in wearable e-textile projects. It consists of a smooth back and a series of huge connecting pads. This allows the board to be sewn onto fabrics using conductive thread. It can be paired with other fabric mounted elements, such as actuators, sensors and power supplies, and I/O elements. Some of these fabric-mounted elements are even washable. The LilyPad Arduino board is powered by the ATMEGA168V processor, though some versions use the ATMEGA328V.

Arduino Nano

This is a tiny and complete board that is based on the ATMEGA328 CPU. Some earlier versions use the ATMEGA168. This board was designed specifically for use on breadboards. The Nano does not have a power jack. Instead, it is powered by a mini-B USB cable.

Arduino Pro Mini

The Arduino Mini comes with an ATMEGA328 CPU. It is equipped with 8 analog input pins and 14 digital I/O pins. Of these, 6 are capable of pulse width modulation. The Pro Mini also comes with some extra holes for mounting pin headers, a reset button and an onboard oscillator. The Pro Mini does not have any USB port. However, you can add USB power and communication by connecting it with a Sparkfun breakout board or a FTDI cable.

Arduino Fio

This board is powered by the ATMEGA32U4 CPU. It comes equipped with 8 analog input pins and 14 digital I/O pins, of which 6 have pulse width modulation capabilities. The Fio also comes with some holes for mounting pin headers, a reset button and an on-board resonator. You can either power it via USB or using lithium polymer batteries through the provided connections.

This board was designed for wireless applications. You can upload sketches to the Arduino Fio using a Sparkfun breakout board or an FTDI cable. Additionally, it is possible to upload sketches to the Fio wirelessly using a modified USB-to-XBee adaptor. The Fio does not come equipped with pre-mounted headers. However, you can solder wires directly or use various types of connectors.

Arduino Zero

The Arduino Zero development board was developed out of a collaboration between Arduino and Atmel. It was designed to be a simple and elegant yet powerful 32-bit extension to the platform debuted by the Arduino Uno. The aim of the Arduino Zero is to offer a platform for innovative projects in crazy robotics, high tech automation, wearable tech, smart IoT devices, and so much more.

The Arduino Zero is powered by the SMART SAM D21 MCU chip built by Atmel. This chip comes with a 32-bit ARM Cortex M0+ core. The Zero also comes with 32kn SRAM and 256kb of flash memory, as well as compatibility with 3.3V shields. It also comes with Atmel's Embedded Debugger. This gives you a full debug interface on the main MCU chip with no need for separate hardware. The Embedded Debugger also gives you a virtual COM port that you can use to program your board.

Arduino Leonardo Board

The Arduino Leonardo is a simple and cheap Arduino board that uses one microcontroller along with a USB. This board is powered by the ATMEGA32U4 and comes with 12 analog input pins and 20 digital I/O pins, 7 of which have pulse width modulation capabilities. It is also equipped with an ICSP header, a micro USB port, a reset button, a 16 MHz crystal resonator and a power jack. The Leonardo has everything required to run the microcontroller, therefore all you need is to power it using a battery, an AC-to-DC converter, or connect it to a PC via USB and you are good to go. This means that a secondary processor is not required for the Arduino Leonardo. Since it handles USB directly, the Leonardo can be recognized by a PC as a keyboard or mouse, as well as a COM port.

Arduino Shields

Arduino Shields are pre-built circuit boards that act as peripherals to different Arduino boards. By connecting an Arduino board to compatible shields, you can give the Arduino board additional capabilities, such as CD screen controlling, wireless communication, motor controlling, and internet access. There are several different types of Arduino Shields. Some of the most common include:

• Proto Shields

• Ethernet Shields

• GSM Shields

• Wireless Shields

The models discussed above are some of the most common types of Arduino boards. However, you should keep in mind that the Arduino platform, including the hardware, is open source.

As such, some people have tweaked the original designs of some Arduino boards to come with their own variants. This means that there are several other unofficial Arduino boards that you might come across.

Chapter Summary

In this chapter, you learned that:

• You can categorize different Arduino models by processing capabilities, feature-set or form-factor.

• The Arduino Uno is one of the most popular versions of the Arduino, and a good option if you are just starting to experiment with Arduino boards.

• The Arduino Due was the first Arduino board to use a 32-bit ARM core microcontroller chip.

• The Arduino Yun comes with an onboard Linux distribution, wireless connectivity and a micro-SD card slot, combining the ease of Arduino with a powerful networked computer.

• The Arduino Micro was built in collaboration with Adafruit, and comes with a form factor that is well suited for placement on a breadboard.

• The Arduino Robot is essentially an Arduino on wheels that comes with two boards – a motor board and a control board – and a processor for each board.

• The Arduino Esplora was made for people who want to get started with Arduino without any prior knowledge of electronics.

• The Arduino Mini is designed for use on breadboards as well as on projects with space limitations.

• The LilyPad Arduino Board is designed for use in wearable e-textile projects.

• The Arduino Nano is a tiny and complete board that was designed specifically for use on breadboards.

• The Arduino Fio was designed for wireless applications.

• The Arduino Zero development board was developed with the aim of offering a platform for innovative projects in crazy robotics, high tech automation, wearable tech, smart IoT devices, and so much more.

• Arduino Shields are pre-built circuit boards that act as peripherals for adding extra functionality to Arduino boards.

In the next chapter you will learn how to setup the IDE, how to connect your board, and how to upload your first sketch.

Chapter 3: Getting Started With Arduino

In this chapter, you will learn how to connect your Arduino board to your PC, how to configure the IDE, and how to upload your first sketch (program).

As mentioned earlier, the Arduino platform consists of two elements: the physical board and the Integrated Development Environment (IDE). The IDE is what you use to write and upload program code to your board. The Arduino IDE is available both on desktop and online. This chapter will take you through the process of getting started with Arduino both on desktop and online. In this guide, we will be using the Arduino Uno.

Using Arduino On The Arduino Desktop IDE

If you intend to program your Arduino board on desktop, the first thing you need to do is to download and install the Arduino Desktop IDE. You can download the Desktop IDE for free from the Arduino downloads page. Once the program downloads, run it and follow the prompts to install it on your PC. You can also download a ZIP file of the program and install it manually.

Once the Desktop IDE has finished installing, connect your Arduino board to your PC using a USB cable. Connecting via USB powers up the board and allows you to program it. Once you establish the USB connection, the green power LED on the board will turn on to indicate that the board is on.

The next step is to install the drivers for your board. If you installed the IDE using the Installer, the board drivers will automatically install drivers immediately when you connect the board. If you installed the IDE from the ZIP file, you will need to manually install the drivers. To do this, follow the steps below:

• Go to your computer's Start Menu and start the Control Panel.

• In the Control Panel window, find System and Security and open up the System window. From there, click on Device Manager.

• Once the Device Manager window is up, navigate to the 'Ports (COM & LPT)' entry and look for an open port labeled 'Arduino UNO (COMxx)'. If your computer does not have a 'COM & LPT' entry, navigate to the 'Other Devices' entry and look for 'Unknown Device'.

• Once you find 'Arduino UNO (COMxx)', right click on it and select 'Update Driver Software'.

• Select 'Browse My Computer'.

• Navigate to the folder where you extracted the contents of the ZIP fill and look for a folder named 'Drivers'. Open the folder and click on the file named 'Arduino.inf'.

Once you select the driver file, Windows will install the drivers.

Selecting Your Board Type And Port

Before you can upload any sketches on your board, you need to define the board you are using and select the port that will be used to upload sketches to the board. To do this, run the Arduino Desktop IDE and go to the 'Tools' menu. Click on 'Board' to bring up a list of all the connected devices. From this list, select the entry that matches your board.

Go to the 'Tools' menu again and bring up the 'Serial Port' menu. From this, select the serial device of your board. In most cases, this will be COM3 or higher. If you are unsure, disconnect your board and bring up the 'Serial Port' menu once again. If you find that an entry has disappeared, that is the entry that corresponds to your board. Plug in your board and select that entry as your serial port.

Opening Your First Sketch

The Arduino Desktop IDE comes with some example sketches that you can use right off the bat. We are going to use one of these example sketches – the LED blink sketch – to test your board. To open the example sketch, on the Arduino Desktop IDE program, go to 'File' and find 'Examples'. Select '01. Basics' and click on 'Blink'.

Uploading The Program

Once you have opened the Blink example, click on the 'Upload' button. The upload process might take a couple of seconds. During this time, you will notice that the TX RX LED's will be flashing to show that data is being received by the board. Once the upload process is complete, you will see the message 'Done Uploading' on the status bar.

Once the sketch has been uploaded to the board, the orange LED on your board (marked L) will start blinking. Congratulations! You have successfully uploaded your first sketch to your Arduino Board.

Using Your Arduino On The Arduino Web IDE

Apart from the Arduino Desktop IDE, you can also program your board using the Arduino Web Editor. The Web IDE works with all Arduino boards, without the need to install anything. Once you connect an Arduino board, it automatically detects the type of board and configures itself accordingly. Since it is hosted online, the Web IDE is always updated with all the latest features. With the Arduino Web Editor, you can use your web browser (Firefox, Chrome, Edge and Safari) to write programs and upload them to any official Arduino board. I recommend that you use Chrome for optimal performance.

The Web Editor is part of a larger platform known as Arduino Create. This is an online platform where Makers can write code, share projects, configure boards and access Arduino tutorials. It provides a single dashboard from where you can manage all aspects of your project. With Arduino Create, you can also save your sketches on the cloud and access them from any internet connected device.

To get started with the Web IDE, you need to sign up for an Arduino account. To do this, simply head in to the Arduino website and click on the sign up button. Fill the registration form and click on 'Create Account". A confirmation link will be sent to your email address. Clink on the link to activate your account. Apart from giving you access to the Web IDE, the Arduino account allows you to buy products from the Arduino store, to create tutorials, to post on the official Arduino Forum, and to comment on posts on the official Arduino blog.

After activating your Arduino account, login to the Arduino Web Editor by going to create.arduino.cc/editor. When logging in for the first time, you will be required to accept the terms and conditions, after which you will be ready to start using the Web Editor. You will also be given a link to the official Arduino Forum, where you can share your feedback and report any bugs you might come across.

Choosing Your Platform

The Arduino Web Editor is compatible with a number of operating systems. If you are using Mac, Windows or Linux, you will need to install the Arduino Web Editor plugin. Without this plugin, you cannot upload sketches to your board from your web browser. If you are using a Chromebook or Chromebox, you will need to go to the Google App Store to download and install the Arduino Create Chrome App.

Anatomy Of The Arduino Web Editor

Once you log in to the Arduino Web Editor, you will notice that the web app consists of three main columns.

The first column gives you access to the following:

- Your Sketchbook: This section contains all the sketches you have created on the Web Editor.

- Examples: These are read-only sample sketches that come with your Web Editor account. These sketches are meant to help you familiarize yourself with the behavior of the libraries and the basic Arduino commands.

- Libraries: These are pre-written packages that you can add to your sketches for extra functionality.

- Serial Monitor: This is a feature that allows your board to receive and send data through a USB connection.

- Help: This is a collection of useful links as well as a glossary of the most common Arduino terms.

- Preferences: This section allows you to customize the look and feel of the editor to your liking. It allows you to tinker with options such as theme colors, and text size.

When you select any of the menu items on the first column, it will display its options in the second column.

Finally, there is the third column, which is the actual code area. This column allows you to write your sketches, verify them, share them with other Arduino users, save them on the cloud, or upload them to your board.

Uploading Your First Sketch

Now that your online IDE is well set up, it is time to confirm whether your board can communicate with your PC. You will do this by uploading a sketch to your Arduino board. Similar to what we did with the Desktop IDE, we will use the 'Blink' example.

• Before we get started, you can click on 'Preferences' to ensure that the look and feel of the Web Editor is to your liking.

• Connect your Arduino board to your PC using a USB cable. The Web Editor will auto-discover your board and serial port. It will provide you with a dropdown menu from where you can select the board you want to upload your sketch to.

• Click on 'Examples', then select 'Basic' and then click on 'Blink'. This will display the code of the Blink sketch in the third column.

• Click the 'Upload' button to upload the sketch to your board. Once you do this, the buttons will be replaced by a 'Busy' label as the sketch uploads. Once the upload process is completed, the message 'Success: Done uploading' will be displayed.

Once the code has been successfully uploaded to your board, the orange LED on your board (marked L) will start blinking. Congratulations! You have successfully uploaded your first sketch to your Arduino Board using the Web Editor.

In some instances, a new Arduino board might come with the Blink sketch already loaded, so you might be unsure as to whether you are truly in control of your board. To confirm whether you are in control of your board, you can change the delay time on the blink sketch and re-upload the code. If you notice a change in the frequency at which the LED blinks, you can now be certain that you are in control of your board.

Documenting Your Projects

It is always a great idea to document your projects. To understand what project documentation looks like, click on the 'Examples' menu and choose the 'Fade' sketch. You will find a 'schematic.png' and a 'layout.png' tab. These provide illustrations on how to configure your electronics for the 'Fade' sketch. Similarly, you can provide such documentation for your own projects. To do this, click on the last tab of the third column, and click on 'Import File into Sketch'.

Sharing Your Sketches

When you are working on the Wed Editor, a unique URL is assigned to every sketch you create. By clicking on the 'Share' button, you can copy this URL and share it with other Arduino users. By clicking on the link, they can view your code or download it into their Sketchbook. Similarly, you can create a tutorial and share it using its unique link.

Libraries And The Arduino Web Editor

The Arduino Web Editor gives you access to over 700 libraries which have been written by the Arduino community. You can include these libraries in your sketches without the need to install anything. All you need to do is to browse through them within the Library Manager and choose those you like. When you use a library, it is automatically detected by the Web Editor. This allows your code to compile without the need to install the library.

Similarly, if you include libraries in your code and share your sketch with another user, they will be able to copy and use the code without having to install the library. Instead of having to share the library, the Web Editor will simply access the library from Arduino's servers. This eliminates the cumbersome process of sharing a sketch together with its associated libraries. However, this option is not available when using the Desktop IDE. You can also add your own custom libraries by converting them into ZIP files and importing them using the 'Import' button on the Library panel. If you want to add several custom libraries in one go, create a single zip file containing all of the custom libraries you want to add, and then import this file.

Chapter Summary

In this chapter, you learned:

• You need to have access to the Arduino IDE before you can start using your Arduino board.

• The Arduino IDE comes in two versions; the web version and the desktop version.

In the next chapter you will learn how to code for Arduino.

Chapter 4: How To Code For Arduino

In this chapter, you are going to learn what an Arduino sketch looks like, how to create a simple Arduino sketch, and the basic parts of an Arduino sketch.

Arduino uses a coding language that is very similar to C++, one of the most common programming languages in the world. As such, if you have prior programming experience with C++, you will find programming for the Arduino to be very easy, since all the basic concepts remain the same. However, you can easily learn to write code for Arduino, even if you do not have prior programming experience.

Arduino Sketch Structure

Every Arduino sketch consists of two main functions:

void setup() – this is where you write your set up code that will only run once.

void loop() – this is where you write your main code which will run repeatedly until the board is turned off.

To view these two basic functions, run the Arduino IDE and go to 'File', find 'Examples', hover on '01. Basics' and click on 'BareMinimum'. This will open a sketch containing only these two functions. The BareMinimum sketch looks like this:

```
void setup() {
// put your set up code here, to run once:
}
void loop() {
// put your main code here, to run repeatedly:
}
```

Below are a few things you need to know about functions:

• Every function has a unique name. For instance, 'setup' is a unique function name.

• A pair of opening and closing parentheses '()' should come immediately after the function name. These parentheses may or may not contain something.

• Each function is accompanied by a return type. For instance, the return type for the 'setup' and 'loop' functions is 'void'.

• The body of a function is enclosed between an opening and closing brace '{ }'.

You will notice that the terms 'void' and 'setup' or 'loop' appear in different colors. The Arduino IDE does this to differentiate between function names and function return types.

Basic Arduino Code Logic

The basic Arduino code follows an 'IF-THEN' logic. A basic fully-functioning Arduino sketch can be divided into four blocks:

- Setup – This is the part of the code that is written within the setup function we discussed above, which performs activities that will only be required to run once.

- Input – This block is placed at the start of the loop function to read the inputs. The values provided by the inputs will act as the conditions for the 'IF' part of the code logic. For instance, if data from a sensor equals a certain value, then the program should perform a certain function.

- Manipulate data – this block defines how data from the sensors will be used to perform calculations, or converted into a more convenient form.

- Output – This block defines the 'THEN' part of the logic, or the final outcome after data has been read and manipulated by the program. For instance, if a program

28

has been written to turn on the heating system if data from a temperature sensor crosses a certain threshold, turning on the heating system is the output.

Pin Definitions

In many cases, you will need to use the different Arduino pins within your projects. Before you can do this, you need to define the pins you are using and the functionality assigned to each pin. A good way of defining pins is to use the following line:

```
'#define pinName pinNumber'
```

To define the function of the pin, we use the PinMode () method within the setup function. This defines the pin as either an input or output.

Variable Declarations

When using the Arduino, sometimes it becomes necessary to declare variables that will be used by the program later on. A variable basically allows you to define and store a value for future use. For instance, you can define data from a sensor as a variable, and then store it for later use.

Creating Your First Sketch

Now that you know the basic structure of a sketch, let's get down to actually creating your first sketch. In keeping up with programming tradition, we are going to write a 'hello world' program that will show the words "Hello, world!" on the screen. Since the Arduino does not have a monitor to display the text, we are going to use the USB port and serial monitor window.

To create the 'hello world' sketch, go to the 'BareMinimum' sketch and make the following modifications:

```
void setup() {
  Serial.begin(9600);
  Serial.println("Hello, world!");
}

void loop() {
}
```

To save your modified program, go to 'File' and click on 'Save As'. Rename the program to 'hello_world'.

To run the program, you first need to upload it to your Arduino board. Connect your board to the PC via USB and click on the upload button. To view the results of the program, open the Arduino IDE Serial Monitor window by clicking on the button that looks like a magnifying lens on the top right side of the IDE. You should be able to see the "Hello, world!" text on the serial monitor window.

Programming Errors

If you make a mistake when typing in the above lines of code, it will result in a compile error. Therefore, you need to make sure that you have typed your code exactly as it is shown above. The IDE compiles your program whenever you click on the 'Verify' or 'Upload' buttons. If there is mistake in your code, the IDE will display a compile error at the bottom of the code area, along with a description of the mistake that caused the error.

Setup Faults

Sometimes, you might encounter some problems when trying to upload sketches to your board. In this case, you need to ensure that you have selected the correct board. To do this, go to 'Tools' and click on 'Board'. Check whether you have actually selected the correct board. From there, go to 'Tools' and click on 'Serial Port' to check whether the correct serial port is selected.

Baud Rate Setting Fault

Sometimes, you might upload your sketch to your board successfully but still be unable to view the display text on the serial monitor window. This could be as a result of an incorrect baud rate setting. Check this setting at the bottom right corner of the serial monitor window, and ensure that it is set to 9600 baud.

Arduino Sketch Program Flow

Whenever you run an Arduino sketch, the individual lines of code (also known as statements) are executed in order from top to bottom. If you want to change this top-to-bottom execution, you need to use flow control statements.

To understand how statements in an Arduino sketch are executed, let us take a look at how the 'hello world' sketch works. Since the 'setup()' function appears first, the statements within this function will be the first to be executed. The first statement within the function is 'Serial.begin(9600)', so it is the first one to be executed. This statement tells the program that is should use 9600 baud as the speed of the serial port. In order for the board and the serial monitor window to communicate at the same speed, the baud setting on the serial monitor window should be set at 9600.

Once the 'Serial.begin(9600)' statement has been executed, it is followed by the 'Serial.println("Hello, World!")' statement. This statement tells the serial monitor window to display the "Hello, World!" text. The 'Serial.println(" ")' statement instructs the serial monitor window to display whatever text is in between the opening and closing quotation marks.

Remember, we said that the 'setup()' function is executed only once. This applies to all the statements within the 'setup()'

function. From there, the program will move on to the statements within the 'loop()' function.

The program runs immediately when it is uploaded to the Arduino board. When you open the serial monitor window, it resets the board, causing the program to run again. You can also rerun the program by pressing the reset button on your board or by unplugging and re-plugging in your board.

Statements in the 'loop()' function are also executed in the same top-to-bottom order. However, once the last statement has been executed, the program loops back to the first statement and repeats the execution. For instance, if there are two statements in the 'loop()' function, the program will execute the first statement, then the second, then the first, then the second, and so on. This continues until the program is stopped.

In our 'hello world' sketch, we do not have any statements in the 'loop()' function. When the program execution gets here, it will get stuck since there is nothing to do. It is important to include a 'loop()' function in your sketch, even if it contains no statements. Without the 'loop()' function, the board will try to run any instruction it finds in memory. By including a 'loop()' function, program execution is kept in the loop, so it won't attempt to move on to other instructions.

Chapter Summary

In this chapter, you learned:

• Every Arduino sketch consists of two main functions, the 'setup' function and the 'loop' function.

• The basic Arduino code follows an 'IF-THEN' logic.

• A basic, fully-functioning Arduino sketch can be divided into four blocks: setup, input, data manipulation, and output.

• The individual lines of code in an Arduino sketch are executed in order from top to bottom.

• You created your first Arduino sketch.

In the next chapter you will learn how to create some simple Arduino projects.

Chapter 5: Simple Arduino Projects You Can Try Out

In this chapter, you will learn how to build a few easy Arduino projects that are perfect for beginners just getting started with Arduino. These projects will also increase your basic understanding of the Arduino platform, both the hardware and the software. Before you can get started with these projects, you should have already downloaded the Arduino IDE and configured it as shown in Chapter Three.

To complete these projects, you will need some components, such as an Arduino board, a breadboard, some LED's and buttons, resistors and some jumper wires. Luckily, you can get most of these items by purchasing any of the several Arduino starter kits that are available on the market.

Before we get started, let's take a short look at the breadboard. A breadboard is a basic prototyping tool that is very useful for testing different wiring and circuit designs without having to solder together the different parts of your circuit. Since most Arduino projects involve a lot of experimentation, using a breadboard will save you a lot of time and material. After you are satisfied with your circuit design, you can then create a printed circuit board or create your circuit on a perforated prototyping board. We are going to use a breadboard in the majority of the projects discussed in this chapter.

Project 1: Blink An LED

This is a very simple Arduino project where we are going to use your Arduino board to blink an LED connected to the board. In this project, you will need the Arduino Uno board, a half-size breadboard, a 5mm LED, a USB cable, some jumper wires, and a 220 Ohm resistor.

Connecting Your Components

Once you have your components ready, you need to connect them to form a working circuit. To help you determine the exact point where you need to connect each component, we are going to use a letter/number combo to identify the location on the breadboard. For instance, if I mention F7, I am referring to a location situated on the seventh row of column F.

Connect your components by following the steps below:

• Take a black jumper wire and insert one end into the GND pin on your board. Insert the other end of the wire into row 15 of the GND rail on your breadboard.

• Take a red jumper wire and insert one end into pin 13 of your Arduino board. Plug the other end of the wire into F7 on your breadboard.

• Plug the LED's LONG LEG into H7, and plug the SHORT leg into H4 on the breadboard.

• Take your 220 Ohm resistor, bend one leg, and insert it into row 4 of the GND rail on the breadboard. Bend the other leg and insert it into row 14.

Your circuit is now complete. Connect your Arduino board to your PC via USB.

Uploading The Blink Sketch

The next phase of this project is to upload the blink sketch onto your Arduino board. Instead of creating a new sketch from scratch, we are going to use the sample sketches that come pre-written in the Arduino IDE. To open the blink sketch, run the Arduino IDE and click on 'File'. Navigate to 'Examples', choose 'Basic' and then select 'Blink'. This will load up the blink sketch on the code area of your IDE. Before uploading the sketch onto your board, you need to verify it by clicking on the check mark button on the top left of the IDE. Clicking on this button tells the program to compile the sketch and check for errors. Once it is done compiling, it will give the message 'Done Compiling'. You can now upload the sketch to your board by clicking the upload button.

As the sketch uploads, you will notice the RX TX LED's on your board flashing rapidly. Once the upload is complete, the sketch will start executing. The LED on the breadboard will start flashing in a continuous loop at intervals of one second.

Project 2: LED With Switch

Now that you have successfully blinked an LED using your Arduino board, let's take things a step further and introduce a switch. A switch is an electrical component that allows you to easily complete and break electric circuits by pushing and releasing it. In this project, we will control an LED using a small push button switch. For this project, you will require the Arduino Uno board, a half-size breadboard, a 5mm LED, a push button switch, some jumper cables, a 220 Ohm resistor, and a 10k Ohm resistor.

Connecting The Components

Connect your components by following the steps below:

• Take a blue jumper wire and connect one end to the GND pin on the Arduino board. Connect the other end into the GDN rail on your breadboard, next to A13.

• Take another blue jumper wire and connect one end into the GND rail on the breadboard, next to A17. Connect the other end to H19.

• Using a red jumper wire, connect H26 on the breadboard to the power rail, somewhere around row 27.

• Using a green jumper cable, connect J24 on the breadboard to pin 2 on your Arduino board.

• Bend one leg of the 10k Ohm resistor, and plug it into G19 on the breadboard. Bend and plug the other one into G24.

• Connect the push button switch to E24, E26, F24, and F26.

• Bend one leg of the 220 Ohm resistor, and plug it into G5 on the breadboard. Bend the other one and plug it into D5.

• Plug the LED's short leg into the GND rail on the breadboard, near A5. Plug the other leg into B5.

• Using a black jumper wire, connect pin I5 on the breadboard to pin 13 on your Arduino board.

• Take another red jumper wire and plug one end into the 5V pin. Plug the other end into the power rail on your breadboard, in a location near A8.

Your circuit is now complete. Connect your Arduino board to your PC via USB.

Uploading The Switch Sketch

The next phase of this project is to upload the switch sketch to your Arduino board. Again, we will be using one of the sample sketches that come pre-written in the Arduino IDE. To open the switch sketch, in the IDE environment, go to 'File', navigate to 'Examples', click on 'Digital' and select 'Button'. This will load the switch sketch onto the code area.

Like we did in the previous project, click on the verify button to compile the sketch and check for errors. Once the compilation is complete, upload the sketch to your Arduino board.

Once the sketch has finished uploading to the Arduino board, you should be able to turn the LED on and off by pressing the push button.

Project 3: Traffic Light Controller

This is another simple project that will advance the knowledge you have gained so far. In this project, you are going to use a green, yellow, and red LED to mimic a traffic light on your breadboard. This project will also take your skills a notch higher by allowing you to create your own code instead of relying on the prewritten code that comes with the Arduino IDE. For this project, you will require an Arduino board, green, yellow, and red LED's, a breadboard, some jumper wires, six 220 Ohm resistors, and a 10K Ohm resistor. You can complete this project with most versions of the Arduino board, as long as your model has enough pins.

Connecting Your Components

Using the jumper wires and a 220 Ohm resistor, connect digital pins 8, 9, and 10 of your Arduino board to the LONG leg of each LED. Connect the SHORT legs of each LED to the GND rail on your breadboard. Using a jumper wire, connect the GND rail to the GND pin on your Arduino board.

The Code

The first thing we will do is to define the variables for this sketch. This will allow us to use names instead of numbers to address the lights. Run your Arduino IDE, create a new project, and write the following lines:

```
int red = 10;
int yellow = 9;
int green = 8;
```

The next step is to create the setup function. This function will configure the LED's as your outputs. If you have already created the variables through the previous step, you can now address the pins by name in the next section. Create the setup function as follows:

```
void setup(){
    pinMode(red, OUTPUT);
    pinMode(yellow, OUTPUT);
    pinMode(green, OUTPUT);
}
```

Now comes the challenging part – creating the logic that will run the traffic lights. To do this, add the following code to your sketch.

```
void loop(){
    changeLights();
    delay(15000);
}

void changeLights(){
    // green off, yellow on for 3 seconds
    digitalWrite(green, LOW);
    digitalWrite(yellow, HIGH);
    delay(3000);

    // turn off yellow, then turn red on for 5 seconds
    digitalWrite(yellow, LOW);
    digitalWrite(red, HIGH);
    delay(5000);

    // red and yellow on for 2 seconds (red is already on
though)
    digitalWrite(yellow, HIGH);
    delay(2000);

    // turn off red and yellow, then turn on green
    digitalWrite(yellow, LOW);
    digitalWrite(red, LOW);
    digitalWrite(green, HIGH);
    delay(3000);
}
```

Once you add the above blocks of code, your program is now complete. Like the previous projects, click on the verify button to compile the sketch and check for errors. Once the compilation is complete, upload the sketch to your Arduino board. Once you have successfully uploaded your traffic light sketch to your board, you will have created a mini traffic light system, with the lights changing every 15 seconds.

Project 4: A Pedestrian Crossing

Now that you have successfully created a traffic light, let's take things a step further by adding a push button that pedestrians can press to change the light whenever they want to cross the road. For this project, in addition to the components you used for the traffic light, you will need a push button switch. Connect the components the same way you did for the traffic light. Connect digital pin 12 to one leg of the push button switch.

Connect the push button switch to E19, E21, F19, and F21. Connect the 10 Ohm resistor to I19, and I25. Using a jumper wire, connect J25 to the GND rail on your breadboard. The 10k Ohm resistor acts as a pull-down resistor. Usually, a switch is meant to allow or cut off the flow of electric current. However, in a logic circuit, there should always be a continuous flow of current, either in a low or high state. When the push button switch has not been pushed, you might assume that the switch is in a low state. However, the switch is actually 'floating', since it is drawing no current.

In this floating state, fluctuations of electrical interference might lead to false readings. This means that the floating switch will not give a reliable low or high state reading. To prevent this, a pull-down resistor is used. It ensures that a tiny amount of current is flowing when the switch has not been pushed, thus giving a definite low state reading.

In the previous project, the loop function was configured to keep the lights changing every 15 seconds. In this project, we will change loop function to read the state of the push button switch, so that the change of lights will be triggered by the push button.

The Code

The first thing we will do is to add a new variable to the program. Do this by adding the following line to your traffic light sketch:

```
int button = 12; // switch is on pin 12
```

We will also change the set up function by adding a new line that configures the switch as an input. We will also add a new line that sets the default state of the traffic lights as green. Without this line, the traffic lights will remain off until the push button switch is pressed for the first time. The two lines we are going to add to the setup function are:

```
pinMode(button, INPUT);
digitalWrite(green, HIGH);
```

We are then going to replace the entire loop function with the following code:

```
void loop() {
    if (digitalRead(button) == HIGH){
        delay(15); // software debounce
        if (digitalRead(button) == HIGH) {
            // if the switch is HIGH, ie. pushed down - change
the lights!
            changeLights();
            delay(15000); // wait for 15 seconds
        }
    }
}
```

With that, your pedestrian crossing sketch is ready. Upload the sketch to your Arduino board. Once the sketch has been uploaded successfully, the green LED will immediately turn on. From there, the lights will change every time the push button switch is pushed.

Chapter Summary

In this chapter, you learned how to create some simple Arduino projects.

Conclusion

Thank you for taking the time to read this book.

By now, I hope that you have gained a thorough understanding of the Arduino platform and how you can use it to come up with all kinds of exciting electronics projects. With a price tag of only a few bucks, you can get started with Arduino for next to nothing!

I hope that after reading this book, you have been inspired to join the thousands of creatives who are using Arduino to come up with all manner of projects. The huge community of Arduino users also means that you will hardly ever get stuck. There are several online forums where you can post your challenges and instantly get help from other Arduino users.

Best of luck as you set out to explore the possibilities presented by the Arduino platform!

www.ingramcontent.com/pod-product-compliance
Lightning Source LLC
Chambersburg PA
CBHW060930050326
40689CB00013B/3035

9 781925 989144